MW01137253

If I Had an Old House on the East Coast

Words by Wanda Baxter
Art by Kat Frick Miller

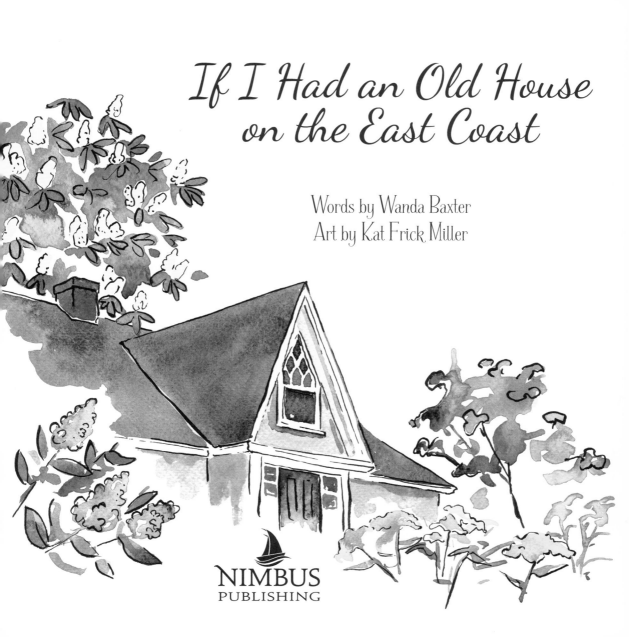

NIMBUS
PUBLISHING

Text Copyright © 2018, Wanda Baxter
Artwork Copyright © 2018, Kat Frick Miller

All rights reserved. No part of this book may be reproduced, stored in a retrieval system or transmitted in any form or by any means without the prior written permission from the publisher, or, in the case of photocopying or other reprographic copying, permission from Access Copyright, 1 Yonge Street, Suite 1900, Toronto, Ontario M5E 1E5.

Nimbus Publishing Limited
3660 Strawberry Hill Street, Halifax, NS, B3K 5A9
(902) 455-4286 nimbus.ca

Printed and bound in Canada

NB1305

Author and Illustrator photos: Callen Singer Photography
Design: Jenn Embree

I have treasured Lizzie Napoli's If I had a Mas in Provence *since I found it in a small shop in Avignon, France, years ago, and it is one of the inspirations for this book. Thanks to her for her beautiful way of seeing, and for the inspiration. –Wanda Baxter*

Library and Archives Canada Cataloguing in Publication

Baxter, Wanda, 1969-, author
If I had an old house on the East Coast / text by Wanda Baxter ; art by Kat Frick Miller.
    Issued in print and electronic formats.
    ISBN 978-1-77108-577-9 (hardcover).—ISBN 978-1-77108-578-6 (HTML)
1. Home economics. 2. Dwellings—Maintenance and repair. 3. Interior decoration. I. Miller, Kat Frick, illustrator II. Title.

TX145.B39 2018   640   C2017-907963-8
                                           C2017-907964-6

Nimbus Publishing acknowledges the financial support for its publishing activities from the Government of Canada through the Canada Book Fund (CBF) and the Canada Council for the Arts, and from the Province of Nova Scotia. We are pleased to work in partnership with the Province of Nova Scotia to develop and promote our creative industries for the benefit of all Nova Scotians.

Old houses, I thought, do not belong to people ever,
not really, people belong to them.

–GLADYS TABER

Love at First Sight

If I had an old house on the East Coast I would fall in love at first sight.
It would grab me by the heart, and not let go.

It would appear as in a dream,
    at the top of a lane,
        with maple trees lining the way.

Below it, a field of hay slopes down, blown sideways in the wind.
    And a brook, too wide to jump,
        meanders through ferns and towering white pine.

In the mornings I'd sit there and drink coffee with the cats and wonder about the place—
how it came to be this way, out of wilderness.

There might be a time-worn photo left behind of the property taken from above:
    a bird's-eye view of the house and old barn, the apple, pear, and cherry trees out behind,
    the ocean barely visible in the distance.

If I had an old house I'd want to find out who lived here before me,
    and who lived here before that,
    all the way back to the original property deed.

I might have a plaque made for the entryway that lists
    the names and dates of the owners of the house over time,
    and recognizes the Mi'kmaq people, who inhabited this region first.

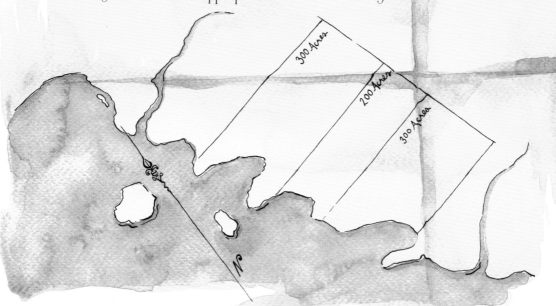

At the Entrance

...would be a stairway of long, thick pieces of slate,
carefully positioned and mortared into stairs.

And on the wooden door, a large heavy knocker, hand-hammered, like
something you might see on an old castle.

I'd want a bright-coloured screen door in its place in the summer
    to let the light in, and the breeze,
    and to mark the end of winter.

A driftwood chime might hang in the entryway, making a faraway sound
    that conjures fog, and lighthouses, and seals.

And if I had an old house on the East Coast, there would be souvenirs
   of visits to the beach, of shells and favourite stones, at the entrance.

I'd keep a bottle for collected sea glass just inside the door,
   where I would drop newly found pieces from my pocket
   when I came home.

This Old House Could Use Some Colour

If I had an old house on the East Coast, I'd want it to burst with bold colour to counter the greys of winter.

Yellow-orange accents on royal blue walls, maybe; defiant and visible, like buoys on the sea.

Moss Green

Red Ochre

French Blue

Yellow Ochre

And inside, I picture a more traditional appearance, of muted heritage colours on interior walls...

...while others would have the crispness of whitewash.
Clean and bright, it lifts the darkness of low ceilings,
wooden beams, and floors.

A Recipe for Whitewash

hydrated lime (not garden lime)

paint brushes

table salt (coarse is best)

water

a bucket

HYDRATED LIME

eye protection

gloves

a stirrer

Optional: some people add molasses as an adherent

Method:

Wearing eye protection, carefully and slowly add 5 parts water to a 5:1 ratio of lime and salt in a deep bucket until it forms a nice paste (if too thin, add a bit more lime).

Paint your walls until beautifully white. Add a coat or two until the colour is even and opaque so it lasts a long time.

If these Old Walls Could Talk...

they would tell stories of the past, of tougher times lived before now.

Under one layer of wallpaper is another layer; under that, another layer—maybe ten layers of wallpaper tell stories of the people who lived here, and of the styles gone by.

birchbark

wooden boards

horse hair

These walls could talk of drafts and wind, and of makeshift insulation: birchbark behind the boards of a wall. Horsehair and straw in the plaster. Thick walls and small windows meant to keep the cold out, and the warmth in.

How to Make and Use a Wall Stencil

Before wallpaper existed, people made decorative wall designs by hand, through a slow and tedious process. If I had an old house, it would seem fitting to try.

1 Find a shape or simple design you like and that would make a nice, repeated design on the wall.

2 Cut out the traced design. Get as tight and clean into the corners as you can so the paint can get into the edges of the design too.

3 Measure out and mark on the wall where you want the stencilled design to go.

4 Hold the stencil tight against the wall with one hand, and paint the stencil in with the other. A small, fine-tipped brush is good for getting into the corners.

5 Keep the stencil in place for a few seconds to let the paint establish, and then remove the stencil carefully. And behold your lovely design. (Hopefully. Or wipe it off quickly, and try again.)

6 Move on to the next marked spot and stencil transfer. Continue until you have a beautiful, hand-stencilled wall that will make you well up with pride.

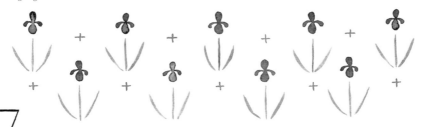

7 Likely, never stencil a wall again. But love that you did it once.

If these walls could talk, they would have hundreds of stories to tell. Of the people who lived here: their struggles, their happinesses, their dreams, their secrets, and their tragedies.

They are here in the palpable silence of nighttime.

And if these walls could talk, it just might be a ghost.

How to Clear your Old House of Ghosts

There are different schools of thought on "clearing" an old house of ghosts, but if you have a ghost, or think you might, here are a few ideas to try:

1 Walk around the perimeter of the house, dropping salt as you go. Think positive thoughts.

2 Perform a "smudging" (an Indigenous tradition of acknowledging the spirit). With respect, burn sage and welcome positive spirits to watch over your house.

3 Apply the "Learned from the Movies" approach: Talk to the ghost. Tell them they are dead and don't live here anymore, and that it's time to go somewhere else. Be firm, but nice.

4 Invite a professional "clearer," a religious or other spiritual person, to perform a ceremony at your house.

5 Live with the ghost and enjoy them. Ghosts can be funny, and are sometimes good company.

6 When in doubt, do all of the above.

It is a biography of sorts, an old house.

It is the story of a place and its history told through
    what remains of the past:
    square-headed and flat-sided nails, an old, rolled-clay ink pot,
    rusted horseshoes, the butt of a wooden rifle, broken bits of pottery,
    a piece of barbed-wire fence embedded within a tree.

The hand-hewn beams of the ceiling, the huge firebox of chiselled stone
in the centre of the house (kept going throughout winter), a
dormant well dug deep into the back hill. Property lines made of
hand-piled stone, planted hawthorn and poplar trees.

Foundations were built of large chunks of rock, piled one on top of the
other above eye level. Dark and cool, they served as root cellars,
and for storing preserves, cider, syrup—and wine.

If I had an old house it would need renovations—as all old houses do.

Whatever updates were needed, I would make changes that match the style and aesthetic of the old.

It might seem like an impossible fix—say, discovering a steel support beam smack in the middle of a room when you tear out a closet. But it's just time for creative design.

How to Disguise a Support Beam

1 Step back from the support beam and imagine ways you might disguise it. Sketch out options.

← support beam

add shelves

2 Pick your preferred option and refine the design. Let's say you choose an open, zen-like bookcase that lets light through the room.

3 Build a rectangular wooden frame around the support post. Build a wooden frame to match it a few feet away.

4 Affix 3 or 4 pre-stained wooden shelves between the new structures. Stain the rest to match.

5 Forget the beam was there.

In the main room, a fireplace with a bake oven might seem almost
    miraculous: round-edged, pre-industrial bricks shaped into an upside-
    down U. An igloo of bricks, it enables a big roaring fire that, when
    burned down to ash, becomes a bake oven.

We might use it to make brick-oven pizza or roasted vegetables, or,
    as an old house compels, homemade bread.

I Dream of a Kitchen

...with bright sunlight pouring in through a
white, lace-edged curtain in the mornings.

The kitchen would be the heart of the place, as it always was.
  With a deep porcelain sink, a mosaic design of broken pottery
  pieces or sea glass for a backsplash, and an open seating area
  for many to gather around.

Cast iron pans, a copper stove hood, an old butchers' block,
  the kitchen would be a place of cooking and eating together—
  and for squeezing in tight for parties, of course.

There Would be Room to Grow

If I had an old house, there would be old gardens to bring back to life,
and there would be room for more to grow.

That first year, watching all the plants come in (not knowing what
will), would be the most exciting.

The yellow flowers of forsythia bushes might bloom first.
And then, a surprising clump of pasque flower (or prairie crocus)
comes in next, a mauve-purple early burst of spring.

Then the bold, red-orange Asian poppies might bloom;
the perfume and blooms of lilac at the fenceline.

Then come the crocus and daffodils and the jaunty-headed tulips.
And the showy rhododendrons burst open.

Then come the short purple lilies, flowering ground phlox
in the lawn, and the majestic blooms of wisteria, purple
and white, hanging like garland from the pergola.

Maple "helicopters" spin down, dandelions take over the
lawn, and sprawling clumps of white and purple violets
open out to the sun.

The cherry trees, apple trees, and strawberries blossom.
Amaryllis, quince, and the first show of wild rose.
Then raspberry, blackberry, and blueberry bushes bloom,

How to Make Rosehip Jelly

I love that rosehip jelly is made from the fruit of rose bushes, usually left unnoticed and unused (except by birds). Rosehips are delicate looking and tasting, barely pink to light orange-coloured, depending on when they're picked. The earlier, the more delicate the jelly; the later, the more flavourful and complicated.

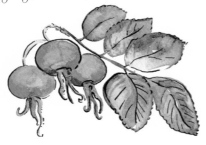

1 Pick rosehips. I tend to pick at the edge of beaches, where rose bushes are heavily fruited and rosehips are big and juicy. Gloves are a good idea because of the thorns.

2 Put rosehips into a large pot and add water to cover. Heat until boiling, and keep boiling. Add water as needed (don't let them boil dry!).

3 When rosehips are soft enough to squish, use a potato masher to mash them down. If there is not much water, boil more and pour it over until mash is more wet than solid.

4 Put entire mass in cheesecloth and tie up overnight, letting it drip slowly through the cloth into a large bowl. Take the juice that remains and pour it through cheesecloth again.

5 Measure juice and put in a large pot. Add twice the amount of sugar. (Gasp! Yes. Jelly is very sweet, as it should be.) Bring to a boil, but just for a minute. Remove from heat. Add pectin and a little lemon juice, and pour into prepared jelly jars. Notice how beautiful it looks, and try a little. Process jars so jelly stays unspoiled a long time.

6 When jars cool, affix lovely labels and, if very keen, cut a nicely patterned paper to put between the lid and the screw top. This delicious jelly deserves to look beautiful.

Then come the hollyhocks in pale yellow and blush pink, their petals near transparent in the sunlight.

And the fluorescent-orange California poppies that bloom and bloom and bloom.

The Russian sage, monk's head lilies, mounds of lavender bushes, the burgundy heather—the flowers would keep coming through until the fall.

How to Make a
Grapevine Wreath with Dried Flowers

Grapevine wreaths are perfect decorations for old houses, to hang on a gate or a door, or inside, or to make into a gift.

1 Prune about 8 to 10 pieces of grapevine, each 6 to 8 feet long. Cut in the dormant season, from October to April, when the vine is woody and doesn't weep. Pull any leaves and fruit off, but be careful to leave decorative tendrils attached.

2 Organize vines into a large, untangled circle. Wind and tuck in ends to secure the circle.

3 Twist 2 or 3 outer vines loosely around and around the larger bunch of vines and tuck wayward vine ends in.

4 Use dried lavender, herbs, berries, heather—whatever you have in your garden—and attach to the vine with wire or its own stem.

5 Hang the wreath on the door of a bathroom or bedroom, or anywhere that could use a sweet decoration. Or wrap in tissue and give as a gift.

If I had an old house I would want to plant vegetables in the old plot behind the barn, nearly overgrown with hay.

Bordered with old gooseberry bushes, black currant, wild roses, and late raspberries, it would need to be dug out and heavily fed, and then re-populated with peas and beans, carrots, onions, garlic, and turnip. Cabbage, asparagus, and squash. Strawberries and tomatoes.

A garden obelisk of collected driftwood would stand in the middle for pole beans and sweet peas to grow on.

How to Grow Zucchini

If I had an old-house garden, it wouldn't seem right not to have zucchini.

1 Form flat-topped mounds of good soil. Plant a few zucchini seeds in each mound.

2 Water proliferously on a regular basis.

3 Be surprised at how fast zucchini grows and how many you end up with.

4 Learn as many ways to eat zucchini and use them in baking as you can.

5 Give zucchini away to most people you know and, potentially, offer them to strangers.

And Nature Surrounds

If I had an old house on the East Coast, I'd want to live on the edge
of nature, where you can see the stars clearly at night.

I would hang a horseshoe above the barn door, turned upward for
    collecting luck, Or downward for spreading luck,
    depending on who you ask,

Water barrels would collect water from the roof for the gardens.

Viceroy

White Admiral

Atlantis Fritillary

Tiger Swallowtail

Monarch

I would want it to be a home not just for
people, but for the wild creatures too.

I would entice barn swallows with nest boxes,
monarch butterflies with milkweed,
and bats with a house of their own.

I would plant more fruit trees, nasturtium, bee balm and butterfly bush to attract bees, butterflies, and birds. And I would let the neon green-headed spit bees build tiny piles of dirt burrows at the bottom of my stairs—and make sure to avoid them through the summer.

I'd hope to see porcupines, groundhog, deer, skunk, and raccoons.

If lucky, I might even see a bobcat sunning itself in the field at the back of the orchard on a late summer afternoon.

How to Make Maple Syrup

If I had an old house on the East Coast I would want
to make maple syrup—like people have for centuries,
once they knew it was sweet. One story goes that a young boy saw a
squirrel drinking sap from a broken branch one day, and so he tried it too.

1 First, you need sugar maple trees, and
syrup-making supplies.

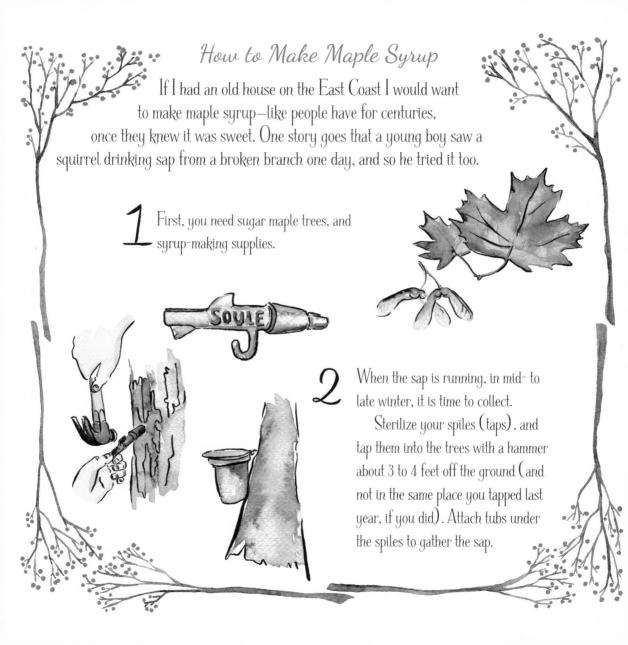

2 When the sap is running, in mid- to
late winter, it is time to collect.
Sterilize your spiles (taps), and
tap them into the trees with a hammer
about 3 to 4 feet off the ground (and
not in the same place you tapped last
year, if you did). Attach tubs under
the spiles to gather the sap.

3 Gather the sap into a larger container at least once a day, and get boiling it as soon as you can. Be prepared to wait around while the sap boils. The sap is mostly water (about 97 percent) and it boils down to a few scant bottles by the time you're done. In the end, though, you'll have the most delicious, rich, sweet syrup you can dream of.

Maple Syrup

4 Filter and then pour the hot syrup into sterile, clean bottles, put labels on, and voila! You're ready.

5 Make pancakes.

If I had an old house, it would seem as though waiting for a chicken coop and the meandering of coo-ing birds.

And if it were a home for chickens,
    I'd want it to be a collection of heritage breeds
    that have resistance to disease, and are
    fantastically strange-looking.
    They would lay eggs of varying sizes and colours,
    and ramble free range through their days.

A Celebration of Harvest

If I had an old house on the East Coast, Thanksgiving would
truly be a celebration of the harvest, eating outdoors with
friends, family, and music.

It would be a hodgepodge of people, young and old, family and
friends, friends of friends, and neighbours—
all contributing something delicious.

We would set up tables across the front yard above the hayfield,
   where the sun would still shine gold late into the day.
It would be nice to have red-and-white-checkered tablecloths, maybe;
   a collection of mismatched cloth napkins, cutlery, and plates.

There would be newly pressed apple cider, older fermented cider, and a variety of wines to share.

Someone would need to be in charge of the turkey— or turkeys, depending on numbers.

And there would be games on the lawn before dinner for people not in the kitchen. Bocce, maybe. Or soccer. Croquet, if people have the patience for hitting balls through small, upside-down hoops.

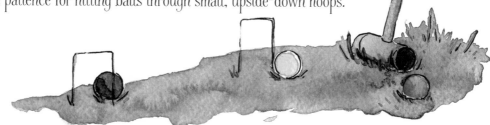

There would be late raspberries growing in October,
    so volunteers could go down to the garden and pick berries for dessert.

And dinner would be a celebration of the harvest, of being together.

And we'd give a toast to the old house, and the land it's on,
    and the people who came before us.

And we'd be thankful the old place was made so well that it's still here,
    and still loved.

Battening Down
the Hatches

If I had an old house on the East Coast, it would be a cozy
nest in the winter, a place to cuddle in by the fire and away
from the world.

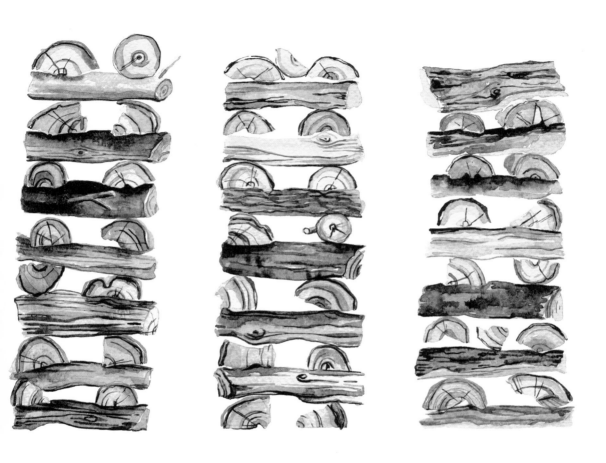

We would have to winterize the gardens first, place firewood in neat
piles in the woodshed, bring in the tools and wrap tender trees,
and put on the storm windows.

But then it would be time to go in,
cozy up, and rest for a while...

...and dream some new dreams, while the snow flies.